THE BOOK OF
THE DAMNED

Also by Daniel Quinn

Ishmael
Providence: The Story of
a Fifty-Year Vision Quest
The Story of B
Beyond Civilization: Humanity's
Next Great Adventure
After Dachau
The Man Who Grew Young
The Holy
If They Give You Lined Paper,
Write Sideways
Tales of Adam
Work, Work, Work
At Woomeroo: Stories
Dreamer
The Invisibility of Success

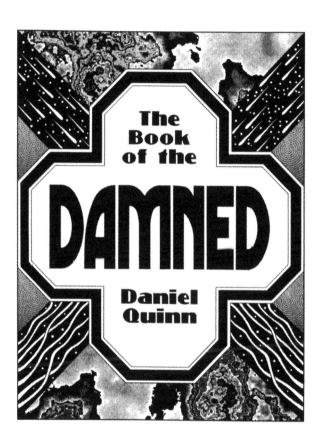

The
Book
of the

DAMNED

Daniel
Quinn

Front cover photo © Valdezrl - Fotolia
Back cover art by the author

ISBN-13 978-1499149999
ISBN-10 1499149999

For Rennie.
Without her,
none of this
would have
happened.

INTRODUCTION

The book for which I am best known, *Ishmael*, came into being over a twelve-year period, beginning in 1979. It was not work on a single book. Rather, it was work on different versions of what eventually became a single book. The first version was *Man and Alien*, the second and third *The Genesis Transcript* (two versions with the same title), the fourth *The Book of Nahash* (from which *Tales of Adam* was later rescued), the fifth *The Book of the Damned*, the sixth and seventh *Another Story To Be In* (again, two versions with the same title), and the eighth at last (and finally), *Ishmael*, the first and only version in which the teacher Ishmael appears.

When I started writing *The Book of the Damned* in 1981, I was sure I'd found the book I was born to write. The versions that came before had been like rainy days with

1

moments of sunshine. THIS was a *thunderstorm*, and the lines crossed my pages like flashes of lightning. When, after a few thousand words, I came to a clear climax, I said, "This MUST be seen," so I put Part One into print.

Parts Two and Three followed, and I began searching for the switch that would turn on Part Four . . . but it just wasn't there. I clung to it for a long time after issuing the first three parts, desperately hoping to find a way to produce additional parts that would bring it to the conclusion I knew was "out there." What I'd done was terrific— and complete in its own way—but at last I faced the fact that *the whole thing just couldn't be done in lightning strikes . . .*

Ten more years passed before I found the way, a completely different way . . . in *Ishmael*, which was the embodiment of my message, providing the foundation for the clarifications, amplifications, and extensions to come in *The Story of B, My Ishmael*, and *Beyond Civilization: Humanity's Next Great Adventure*. But publishing *The Book of the Damned* had been no mistake. It deserved to be published. It still does.

Daniel Quinn, 2014

3

PART ONE

When ecologists find a predictable life-span of a generation separating us from total extinction, it would seem that we have a duty to search for another interpretation of mankind's life story.

—Vine Deloria
God Is Red

WHAT A CURIOUS THING TO SAY.

Because we're on the verge of extinction, we should look for another interpretation of mankind's life story?

What difference does a story make?

It makes a difference. Because the story we have, we are enacting.

We are making it come true.

And in making it come true, we are pushing ourselves toward extinction.

A plant physiologist works to develop a new, more productive strain of wheat that will feed this generation's starving millions.

It's a noble endeavor.

He knows it's a noble endeavor, because he knows that story. What he's doing fits right into it.

He's enacting it; he's making it come true.

But he doesn't know history.

He doesn't need to know history to be a plant physiologist.

So he doesn't know this historical fact: that every increase in food production stimulates a population increase greater than can be supported by that increase in food production. Peter Farb calls it "the basic paradox of food production: intensification of production to feed an increased population leads to a still greater increase in population."

By increasing food production for the starving millions of this generation, the plant physiologist is assuring that there will be even more starving millions in the next generation.

He is enacting the story. He is making it come true.

And the end of that story is the extinction of the human race.

You know the story too. We all do.

We learned it in school.

We learned it in church.

We'd know it even if we never went to school or to church, because every news story, every magazine article, every book is written as a part of that story. Is written with that story as a background. You could learn it just watching television commercials.

You know it.

Think simply.

It's about the conquest of the world. It's about man gaining control over his environment. It's about man rising above nature and mastering it as a workman masters a tool. It's about man reshaping the earth to his own purposes.

That's what the story is about. But what's the story?

You know it.

It has a beginning, a middle, and an end, just like every good story.

The beginning:

Man was born a long, long time ago, about three million years ago. But he wasn't too bright back then; he didn't know he could control his environment. So he had to live pretty much like an animal, just taking whatever came to hand. But time passed and man evolved. *Homo habilis* became *Homo erectus*, and *Homo erectus* finally became *Homo sapiens*— about two hundred thousand years ago.

So there we were. *Homo sapiens*: modern man; clean him up, give him a shave and a haircut and a suit, and he could be a literary critic or a computer programmer.

Then a strange thing happened. For two hundred thousand years, *Homo sapiens* accomplished nothing. Made no effort to gain control of his environment.

God knows why.

Didn't occur to him, probably.

The middle:

Then about ten thousand years ago, *Homo sapiens* finally woke up to the fact that he could control his environment. Instead of living like an animal and depending on whatever came to hand, he could grow his own food. That was the beginning of everything.

Mastery over food supply was the key that unlocked the box of keys. It was the mastery that made all the other masteries possible.

Mastery over food supply meant that man need no longer follow the game as a nomadic hunter-gatherer. He could settle down in one place.

He could build.

He could invent.

He could think.

Mastery over food supply meant that man was free.

Free to conquer the world.
Free to reshape the world to his liking.

The end:
Liberated from the restraints that his environment had imposed on him for three million years, man proceeded to fulfill his manifest destiny. What had once been nomadic camps became villages. Villages grew into towns, towns grew into cities, cities were gathered into kingdoms, kingdoms were gathered into empires. Technology, literacy, government, the arts, the sciences, law, religion, philosophy—all flourished.

It was civilization—the ultimate home of man.

Civilization is the ultimate home of man because, like man, it can never cease to grow —toward an everlasting future of richness, grandeur, enlightenment, and unimaginable accomplishment. Even the stars themselves may not be out of our reach. Perhaps it is our awesome destiny to rule the entire universe.

But that's in the future. Just now we've hit a bad patch right here on earth. We've got to get past that first. We've gobbled up our resources as though they were unlimited. We've got to find more.

So we can go on.

We've devastated the land, poisoned the air, fouled the water. We're on the verge of ecological catastrophe. We've got to fix that.

So we can go on.

Millions of us are starving. A worldwide famine is not out of the question. We've got to increase food production.

So we can go on.

Our population growth is out of control. If it goes on this way, there will be ten billion of us here, maybe twenty billion by the end of the twenty-first century. We've got to get that under control.

So we can go on.

The problem is mastery. We just haven't got enough of it yet. We haven't yet mastered our resources. We haven't yet mastered the ecological processes of the world. We haven't yet mastered food production. We haven't yet mastered population growth.

That's why we have to go on. So we can get the mastery we need. Absolute mastery over everything in the world.

Then it will be paradise.

Then we'll have that everlasting future of richness, grandeur, enlightenment, and unimaginable accomplishment that the story promises us.

This is the story as we learn it. It's ambient in our culture. It's something everyone takes for granted. It's a basic cultural understanding worldwide.

Which is no great wonder.

It's the story of mankind as told by *Homo magister*—Man the Ruler, Man the Master, born in the birth of agriculture.

Wherever *Homo magister* rules, that's the way the story is told. Because that's the way *Homo magister* sees it.

But it's not the only way.

As *Homo magister* tells it, the story of mankind is really a story about him. He's the hero of the story. That's easy to see. In his telling of it, the action only begins when he arrives on the scene. In the three million years before that nothing was happening.

And indeed nothing was happening— so far as *Homo magister* can see. He looks at those three million years and sees a vacancy. Because people weren't mastering anything, and according to *Homo magister* that's what human life is all about.

For all that time, people were just waiting. Waiting to evolve into *Homo magister*.

If it hadn't been for *Homo magister*, people would have gone on doing nothing, getting nowhere.

Homo magister saved the human race from nothingness.

It's true, on the other hand, that if it hadn't been for the arrival of *Homo magister*, millions of people wouldn't be starving today. The earth wouldn't be a cesspool of human wastes. We wouldn't have the capability of destroying the planet at the push of a button. We wouldn't be on the edge of extinction.

But we'd still be shitting in the bushes.

You wouldn't like that, would you?

No bathrooms, no electric blankets, no television, no governments, no churches, no museums, no theaters, no penitentiaries, no schools.

No nothing.

It's silly to think about anyway. Man had to become *Homo magister*. It was man's destiny to become *Homo magister*.

Wasn't it? Well, wasn't it?

What *else* could he have become?

He had to enact this story. Because there was no other story to enact.

And he has to go on enacting this story. Because there is no other story to enact.

This is how *Homo magister* tells the story, because this is the way he sees it.

As told by *Homo magister*, he is the climax of the human story. He is the final product of human evolution. Man may become taller, stronger, or brainier, but he will always be *Homo magister*. It is man's ultimate form.

Even if *Homo magister* topples the ecological balance of the earth, a few will survive. And *Homo magister* will rise from the ashes.

To do it all over again.

Even if *Homo magister* engulfs the world in a nuclear holocaust, a few will survive. That's why we have bomb shelters. So *Homo magister* can rise from the ashes.

To do it all over again.

Because man was divinely appointed to rule the earth.

It's God's problem, really. He made us this way. He made us to rule the world.

It's up to Him to save us.

This is the story *Homo magister* tells about the lifetime of man. It's the story we're enacting.

It's the story that's killing us.

A few hundred years ago, *Homo magister* had

a story he told about the arrangement of the universe. It was a wonderful story, and he was very fond of it. He'd been telling it to himself for more than a thousand years. It had the simplicity of a self-evident truth:

The planet Earth is the center of the universe. Everything in the universe revolves around man's home. Sun, planets, stars, the works.

It has to be that way, because man is the center of the universe. God made the whole thing for man, so obviously He put man in the center of it.

Astronomically speaking, the story didn't work out too well. It was hard to reconcile actual observations with it. But the astronomers did their best, because they too were *Homo magister*. They knew that man belonged in the center of the universe.

Then a madman named Copernicus came along with another story. A story that made sense of the actual celestial observations. He said that the earth isn't in the center of the universe. It isn't even in the center of the solar system. The damned thing revolves around the SUN.

The sun is the center of the solar system.

Homo magister was outraged by this new story. He would have burned the heretic at the stake if he could have, but Copernicus was already safely in the ground.

The next generation of astronomers worked hard to show that the Copernican story was false, but all their observations showed that the Copernican story was nearer the truth than the old Ptolemaic story.

Reluctantly, *Homo magister* was forced to accept the new story. He pretty much had to, because the astronomers were members in good standing of *Homo magister*. If they'd been red Indians, *Homo magister* would have laughed his head off and gone on thinking that the earth was the center of the universe.

The displacement of the earth as the center of the universe was a blow to *Homo magister's* pride. But in the end it saved him from making a fool of himself when he decided to visit the moon. If he had still *[handwritten at top:]* Roman Mathematician / Astronomer believed the Earth to be stationary and the sun & the stars revolving around it

believed that the sun revolves around the
earth, he would have gotten lost.

[handwritten left margin:] Homo magister lost the Ptolemaic view. . . . to compensate for this loss Him. interprets himself to be the center of creation

Homo magister had lost the Ptolemaic story
that placed him at the center of the universe.
This was a disagreeable shock. But he had
another story to fall back on—a story even
older and more venerable than the Ptolemaic
story.

In a way it was even better.

It placed him at the center of *creation*.

When God set out to create the universe,
he hadn't just been killing time. He was
creating the universe so that he could create
something else. He had to create suns and
moons and stars and planets. He had to create
the earth. He had to put air around it and
water in the seas and rivers. He had to create
a complete biological community to live in it,
from earwigs to elephants.

All this had to be done.

So He could create man.

The universe was the home of the planet
earth. And the earth was the home of man,

complete down to the last detail, ready to move into.

It was a turnkey project.

When man's home was all ready for him, God made man.

Naturally, having gone to all this trouble to get man's home ready for its master, God made man so that he was ready to be its master.

Man was BORN *Homo magister*, BORN to rule the earth that had been made for him.

He was born with a box of keys in one hand and a key to the box in the other. The box held all the keys to civilization. The key that opened the box was agriculture.

In other words, so far as *Homo magister* knew:

Man was BORN an agriculturalist and a civilization-builder.

These things were as much innate to him as chirping is to a cricket.

The biological community that God had stocked the earth with was man's food preserve, to be used as suited him. It had no other reason for being there, except to support man's life. If man wanted more cattle in his food preserve, he could breed more cattle. If he wanted the wolves out of his food preserve, he could kill them off.

The biological community of the world had been given to man to use as he would. He wasn't a *part* of that community. Not in any sense.

He was the *ruler* of that community.

He had been born that way.

There wasn't any evidence for this story, of course. People didn't think in terms of evidence in those days. It was simply obvious. Self-evident almost.

It was obvious that civilization was only a few thousand years old. So obviously man was only a few thousand years old. Obviously, then, he'd been born a civilization builder. What *else* could he have been born?

If you had suggested to *Homo magister* then that man had been born a homeless hunter-gatherer and that this homeless hunter-gatherer had lived through three million years without evidencing any inclination toward civilization, he would have laughed at you.

He knew that there were such creatures, of course, in Africa and the New World. And he knew what had happened to them to make them that way. They had degenerated from the natural state. They had lost the key that opens the box of keys.

They had lost the agricultural arts.

They were subhuman, because to be human is to be *Homo magister*. They lived like animals. They were a part of that biological community that had been given to man as his food preserve. Therefore man could do anything he pleased with them. He could hitch them to the plow like oxen or kill them off like wolves.

By virtue of this story, man's place in the universe was secure, even if he wasn't physically at its center. That wasn't important.

He was the end product of creation, the creature for whom all the rest was made.

Having made man, God stopped. Why *wouldn't* He stop?

There was nothing more to make.

It was a wonderful story, an inspiring story.

But then, of course, along came Darwin.

Homo magister detested Darwin a thousand times more than he had detested Copernicus. He would have burned him at the stake if that hadn't gone out of style.

Darwin shattered *Homo magister*'s story of his birth. According to Darwin, man hadn't been born apart from and above the rest of the biological community. He had been born right IN it.

Not its ruler, its product.

Not a master. A subject. Subject to the same biological processes that control the lives of flukeworms and bats and moles.

He had not been shaped by the hand of God. He had been shaped by the mindless forces of natural selection.

He wasn't the son of God. He was the son of apes.

24

He hadn't been born an agriculturalist and a civilization-builder, tall and handsome and brainy. He'd been born a squat, stupid savage. And he'd lived like a savage for hundreds of thousands of years, maybe millions of years. He'd had to pull himself out of the slime.

God had created man in the slime.

Homo magister hated Darwin's story of man's origins. But he had to accept it, at least superficially, because Darwin and all the other biologists who supported the story were members of *Homo magister*. He couldn't ignore it completely. But he could do the next best thing.

He could make it meaningless.

Then he wouldn't have to think about it.

Because you don't have to think about irrelevant, meaningless things.

And so he revised the story of mankind:

Okay, it's true that man was around for three million years or so before *Homo magister* appeared to rule the world.

But that doesn't mean anything.

There's nothing to think about in that.

Because nothing was happening in those three million years. People weren't doing anything.

Because they weren't fully human.

They were biologically human, of course. But they weren't fully human because they weren't accomplishing anything. They weren't *trying* to accomplish anything. They weren't trying to master their environment. Fully human people just naturally want to master their environment. It's innate—in people who are fully human.

Fully human life didn't begin with *Homo habilis* or *Homo erectus* or even *Homo sapiens*. It began with *Homo magister*—with man the agriculturalist and civilization-builder.

With me.

Everything worth knowing I discovered. Everything worth having, I invented. Everything worth doing, I have done.

Nothing people knew before that was worth knowing. Nothing people had before that was worth having. Nothing people did before that was worth doing.

God knew that.

God never spoke to *Homo habilis* or *Homo erectus*. He didn't even speak to *Homo sapiens* for the first two hundred thousand years of his life. God wouldn't waste His time talking to savages.

He was waiting for someone *worth* talking to. Someone fully human. Someone smart enough to recognize the destiny He had set for man. Someone who could appreciate Him. Someone civilized.

He was waiting for me.

In mankind's life story, the two hundred thousand generations that lived and died before me don't count for anything. So you don't have to think about them.

They lived and died for nothing.

Except, in the end, to produce me, the ruler of the world.

Homo magister was ultimately forced to overcome his repugnance to the idea that the earth is not the astronomical center of the universe. To get on with his mastery of the world, he was forced to deal with this repellent idea. He was forced to build a totally new astronomy based on it. If he hadn't, he would have made a fool of himself on the way to the moon.

But he has not yet been forced to deal meaningfully with the fact that his story, the story of man the ruler of the world, represents only a half of one percent of the whole story of man. He hasn't built a totally new understanding of the story based on that fact. He doesn't want to.

But if he doesn't, he's going to make an even worse fool of himself than just getting lost on the way to the moon.

He's going to become extinct.

PART TWO

IT TOOK MAN THREE MILLION YEARS
to figure out that his destiny is to rule the
world.

He was a slow starter.

That's the way *Homo magister*, man the ruler
of the world, tells the story. It's the way he
sees it. The first three million years of human
life were nothing but a long, tedious buildup
to him.

They really could have been dispensed
with. But damned Darwin and his followers
put them there.

So useless. So pointless.

It's like buying a print of the film *Gone
with the Wind* and finding out that it has a
leader three million feet long.

So it's there. So what? Cut it off. Throw
it away.

That's the way *Homo magister* sees it.

He's looked at those three million years, and there's not much more to be seen in them than in the leader to a motion picture. It's like a film made up of a loop endlessly repeating, showing people being born, living for a while, and dying. Over and over again, two hundred thousand times.

Two hundred thousand generations, and not a shred of meaning in any of them.

Futile.

Pathetic.

They might as well not have bothered.

Homo magister understands the people who lived those futile, pathetic lives.

They were what he calls hunter-gatherers.

Definition by occupation.

That's what they did with themselves. Hunted and gathered. Well, why not? They didn't have anything else to do. Such a waste.

If they'd only had the sense to know that they didn't have to live that way—that they could grow their own food instead of hunting it and gathering it—then they could have made something of themselves. Could have started civilization.

Could have become *Homo magister* a lot sooner.

Then their lives would have meant something. Then the real story of man could have gotten started sooner.

Homo magister really sees it that way. He looks at them and sees that their lives were shaped by nothing. By an absence of knowledge. By what they didn't know.

They didn't know that they could grow their own food. So they were stuck with this dumb, dead-end occupation called hunting-gathering.

They couldn't get out of it. Because they just didn't know they could become agriculturalists and civilization-builders.

Which, as everyone knows, is the only truly human way to live.

So when *Homo magister* looks at the history of these people, he naturally perceives it as a void. As nonhistory. How else can you characterize it, except as what was going on before anything happened? It's just before-history. Prehistory.

It's a period of time as empty as the lives that created it. It's empty because nobody was doing anything. Except hunting and gathering. And of course battering stones.

It was the Stone Age.

Definition by product.

Homo magister would naturally see it that way.

But it's not the only way to see it.

Be imaginative.

Forget products. Forget occupations.

Imagine it a different way.

Imagine that our ancestors were enacting a story.

You know what enacting a story is.

We're enacting a story here. A story about man becoming the master of his environment. A story about man's conquest of the world. A story about the fulfillment of man's destiny— as defined by *Homo magister*.

We've been enacting it for some ten thousand years.

Imagine our ancestors enacting a different story from ours. Not a story about man mastering his environment. Not a story about man's conquest of the world. Not a story in which products and productivity figured at all.

Stretch yourself.
Imagine that the story our ancestors were enacting shaped their lives. The way the story we're enacting shapes our lives.

Different stories: different lives.
Imagine that their lives had a different shape from ours because they were enacting a different story from ours.
Go further.
Imagine that enacting their story made their lives meaningful to them. The way enacting our story makes our lives meaningful to us.

Different stories: different meanings.
Imagine that the meaning of their lives was different from the meaning of ours

because they were enacting a different story from ours.

Go further still.

Imagine that enacting their story, generation after generation, gave their history its shape. The way that enacting our story, generation after generation, has given our history its shape.

Different stories: different histories.

Imagine that their history had a different shape from ours because they were enacting a different story from ours.

It's hard, I know, to imagine such things. It would be like asking an eighteenth-century slave-ship captain to imagine that the wretches chained up in his hold were actually human beings like himself, like his wife, like his parents, like his children.

He would have thought you were pulling his leg.

It gets worse.

Think biologically.

Imagine a completely different kind of story from the one we're enacting. A story for the entire lifetime of a genus. The genus *Homo*.

Think of an outline for such a story.

Not three million years of nothingness, followed by an explosive flourishing so violent that it consumes the world in ten thousand years, followed by extinction.

That's not a story for the lifetime of a genus.

Imagine a different story entirely. A story for tens of millions of years. For hundreds of millions of years.

A real story. A story to be enacted.

A story whose enacting shapes the lives of those who enact it.

A story whose enacting shapes the history of those who enact it.

Now imagine that that's the story our ancestors were enacting.

It had nothing to do with mastering the world.

Nobody was trying to master the world.

All of it was about something else.

Stretch yourself.

Imagine that during the first three million years of human life people were enacting a story. And that it was man's destiny to enact that story.

Not just for three million years. For thirty million years.

For three hundred million years.

For the lifetime of our planet, perhaps.

Billions of years.

It was that good a story.

It was a good story, good for the lifetime of a genus.

But it was not a story about power—about conquest and mastery and ruling. Enacting it didn't make people powerful. Enacting it, people didn't need to be powerful. Because, enacting it, people didn't need to rule the world.

Imagine that ruling the world was something they thought they didn't need to do.

Because it was already being done.
As it had always been done.
As it had been done from the beginning.

Imagine that they had a different supposition about the world and man's place in it.

Imagine that they didn't suppose, as *Homo magister* does, that the world belongs to man, that it is his to conquer and rule. Imagine that, in their ignorance, they supposed something else entirely.

Be outrageous.

Imagine that they supposed something completely absurd.

That man belongs to the world.

It was never hidden.

It was only hidden from *Homo magister* because he was sure that what had shaped their lives was nothing—an absence of knowledge, ignorance.

Not something.

Not a different supposition about the world and man's place in it.

Man belongs to the world.

Actually, it's plainly written in their lives. It's plainly written in the general community to which they belonged: the community of life on this planet.

Anyone can read it. You just have to look.

Every creature born in the biological community of the earth belongs to that community. Nothing lives in isolation from the rest; nothing *can* live in isolation from the rest. Nothing lives only in itself, needing nothing from the community. Nothing lives only for itself, owing nothing to the community. Nothing is untouchable or untouched.

Every life in the community is owed to the community—and is paid back to the community in death.

The community is a web of life, and every strand of the web is a path to all the other strands.

Nothing is exempt. Nothing is special. Nothing lives on a strand by itself, uncon-nected to the rest.

Nothing is wasted. Everything that lives is food for another.

And everything that feeds is ultimately itself fed upon or in death returns its substance to the community.

And in belonging to the community, each species is shaped.

By belonging.

By belonging—by feeding and being fed upon, each generation of each species is shaped. Of each generation, some, better suited to survive, live to reproduce. Others, less well suited, do not.

And so the generations are shaped,

By belonging to the community that shapes them.

Nothing is exempt from the shaping.

The fishes that, four hundred million years ago, lived in the off-shore shallows of the oceans were shaped.

And learned to venture up onto the land. And in venturing onto the land were shaped by their contact with the community already living there.

And, being shaped, over millions of years, became reptiles. No longer tied to the shore, the reptiles ventured inland.

Where they were shaped.

So that, over millions of years, some of them became birds. So that some of them, shaped in another way, became mammals.

And the mammals, belonging to a community of plants, birds, amphibians, and reptiles, were shaped. Into many different forms. Into bats and anteaters and dogs and horses and deer and elephants and apes.

And all of these were shaped.

By belonging to the community of life.

By feeding and being fed upon.

And, over millions of years, the members of one branch of the family of apes were shaped into a manlike creature that we call *Australopithecus africanus*.

And *Australopithecus africanus* was shaped over millions of years until he became *Australopithecus robustus*—stronger and taller and still more manlike.

Because he had been shaped. Because he had belonged to the community of life.

And, being shaped over millions of years, *Australopithecus robustus* became still stronger and taller and more manlike, until, looking at him, we have to call him . . . man. *Homo habilis*.

Man was born belonging to the world. Being shaped.

He did not exempt himself from that shaping just because he was man. And so he continued to belong to the community that had shaped him. And, by belonging to it, continued to be shaped.

And, being shaped, *Homo habilis* became stronger and taller and more dexterous and more intelligent, until, looking at him, we have to give him a new name: *Homo erectus*.

And *Homo erectus* was born being shaped, and he belonged to the community that was shaping him.

His life belonged to that community. And those of each generation who were less well suited to survive in the community rendered back their lives at an early age, while the rest lived on to reproduce.

And so *Homo erectus* was shaped, so that

he became stronger, taller, more agile, more dexterous, and more intelligent, until, looking at him, we have to call him . . . us. *Homo sapiens*.

And *Homo sapiens* was born being shaped. He was born a member of the community that was shaping him.

Not exempt from membership by virtue of his greater intelligence. Not isolated from the rest by virtue of his capacity to wonder and dream. Not aloof from the rest by virtue of his knowing that he was unlike the rest in these ways. A part of the rest. And being a part of the rest, *Homo sapiens* was shaped.

Shaped not by nothing. Shaped not by ignorance.

Shaped by belonging to the community of life.

Which was itself being shaped.

The community itself was being shaped.

The matter was being handled.

Not by man.

The shaping of the world was not in man's hands.

It was in other hands, which had shaped it from the beginning.

It was in the hands of the gods.

The gods were shaping the community of life on earth. And man belonged to that community and was being shaped with it and in it.

Man was being shaped by the gods.

Man was living in the hands of the gods. And the gods did not rebuke him. Or send him teachers. Or send him saviors.

Because there was no need to.

Because he was living in their hands.

Man had found his destiny.

He had been fulfilling it from the beginning.

It was his destiny to live in the hands of the gods.

For the lifetime of this planet.

And, following the supposition with which he had been born—the supposition that man belongs to the world—*Homo sapiens* was shaped.

The shaping had hardly begun.

The shaping had hardly begun, but he was already a singer of songs and a dancer and a painter and a sculptor.

The shaping had hardly begun, when, in one part of the world, one branch of the family of *Homo sapiens* said:

Stop.

Man was not born to be shaped.

Man was born to shape.

Man was not born to be shaped by the world. He was born to shape the world.

Stop.

Man was not born to live in the hands of the gods.

Man was born to live in his own hands.

Stop.

We've been testing the wrong supposition.

Man doesn't belong to the world.

The world belongs to man.

It's ours.

To shape.

To conquer.

To rule.

Homo magister had been born. And he
was born refusing to be shaped any further,
refusing to be shaped as man had been
shaped from the beginning—by belonging
to the community of life.

He didn't belong to that community.
That community belonged to him.

He didn't owe his life to it.

It owed its life to him.

He took that life and made himself the
master of it. He took the life of the biological
community into his own hands and used it as
if it belonged to him.

It wasn't a technological advance.

It was a rebellion.

Homo magister would no longer be shaped by
belonging to the community of life. He would
no longer be limited—as all other species are
limited—by that shaping.

He would grow without limit. And to
support that growth, he would reshape the

biological community into his private food preserve.

Food that had once belonged to all he would seize for himself alone, to be shared with no others. Land that had once supported the life of all he would seize for himself alone, to be shared with no others.

This was his right.

If the world belongs to man.

And his growth would be voracious.

Because it was without the limit imposed on all who belong to the community of life.

Homo magister no longer belonged to that community.

And so he grew without limit.

And each growth had to be met with an increase in food production.

And each increase in food production stimulated a population increase greater than could be supported by that increase in food production.

Homo magister was born with his feet on the path to extinction. Because whatever grows without limit necessarily ends by devouring the world.

Homo magister hadn't really escaped the limits imposed on him by the community of life.

He was only outrunning them.

Outrunning them for a little while—for what is only an eyeblink of time in the life of our planet.

For ten thousand years.

The limits caught up with him then.

The limits caught up with him now.

When *Homo magister* is us.

Homo magister doesn't want to hear the story told this way.

He never has wanted to hear it told this way.

He's heard it before, as he carried his rebellion across the face of the earth.

He heard it from those he encountered who were still enacting the old story. From people he called savages because they still belonged to the world. From people he called primitive because they were not at war with the community around them.

They wanted him to understand the story they were enacting. They wanted him to see that it was valuable and important. So he wouldn't make it impossible for them to go on enacting it. So he wouldn't destroy it.

So he wouldn't destroy them.

They didn't know how to explain it so that *Homo magister* would understand. Because they were not of *Homo magister* themselves. They spoke in poetry. They spoke in songs. They spoke in children's stories.

Homo magister listened, sometimes. Sometimes even politely. He didn't understand what they were telling him, of course. He didn't expect to understand anything. What would a savage know that was worth understanding?

But some of what they told him was charming and pretty, and he made a note to save those parts.

Then he went ahead and destroyed them.

They never really had a hope of explaining it, because they didn't belong to *Homo magister*.

They weren't one of his own. Hadn't read the right books. Hadn't gone to the right schools. Hadn't been born and raised to see things from *Homo magister*'s point of view.

So they didn't know how it had to be explained to him.

It really has to be explained to him by one of his own.

Because he really doesn't want to hear it at all.

He doesn't want to look at it. It wouldn't be the first time that *Homo magister* hasn't wanted to look at something.

He didn't want to look at the observations that didn't fit into Ptolemy's picture of the solar system. He didn't want to look at them, because they might mean something. They might mean that man's home was not the center of the universe.

Somebody did it anyway. One of his own.

Damned Copernicus.

Homo magister didn't want to look at the fossil evidence of ancient man. He didn't want to look at it, because it might *mean* something. It might mean that man hadn't been born an agriculturalist and civilization-builder, direct from the hand of God.

Somebody did it anyway. One of his own.

Doubly damned Darwin.

He doesn't want to look now at the first three million years of human life. He doesn't want to look at them, because they might mean something. They might mean that man wasn't born to rule the world—that he was born to do something else entirely.

Somebody is doing it anyway. One of his own.

Triply damned Quinn.

He isn't playing fair.

He isn't talking to scholars.

He's talking to people.

Somebody hang him quick.

PART THREE

GOD IS A SNOB.

When man first appeared in the world, He cut him dead. He took one scornful look at poor, scruffy little *Homo habilis*, then rolled over and went to sleep.

He woke up a couple million years later and had another look. By this time, man was *Homo erectus*. A definite improvement, but still no one God cared to associate with. So He rolled over and went back to sleep.

When He woke up a million years later, He saw that man had become *Homo sapiens*. This was more like it. But as yet *Homo sapiens* was still running around half naked, still just a savage like *Homo habilis* and *Homo erectus*.

So God shrugged and went back to sleep. *Homo sapiens* wasn't ready for him yet.

The next time He woke up, a couple hundred thousand years later—about twelve thousand years ago—He was definitely encouraged. Some progress had been made at last. *Homo sapiens* wasn't quite an agriculturalist yet, but here and there he'd gone a bit beyond pure hunting and gathering.

He was doing a little systematic food-amassing by means of intensive collection. He was harvesting more than he needed from wild crops and storing the excess. He was creating food surpluses.

A good sign. He was beginning to learn how to manipulate his environment so as to increase food production.

God watched his progress with interest for a few millennia. He knew what He was watching: the birth of fully-human man.

Homo magister.

He watched his early, tentative experiments with settlement based on intensive food collection. He watched the population of these settlements grow. Until intensive food collection alone could not support their growth.

So that they were forced to increase food

production: forced to supplement wild crops with crops of their own planting.

Their settlements grew more stable.

More populous.

Until the collection of wild crops, even supplemented by crops of their own planting, was not enough to support their growth.

So that they were again forced to increase food production: forced to convert more and more land to the exclusive planting of their own more productive crops.

To support a population always one step ahead of food production.

It was very inspiring.

Homo magister had crossed a threshold. He had become a true agriculturalist.

And this was about ten thousand years ago.

God was very gratified. Man had at last found the key to the box of keys. But *Homo magister* was only in his infancy. He wasn't ready for God yet.

Soon, God said.

And took a nap for a few millennia. When He woke up, He wasn't disappointed. *Homo*

magister was really on his way now. It
was about 2000 B.C., and the agricultural
revolution had spread throughout Europe.
The early valley civilizations of the Near
East were flourishing. Food production had
increased enormously. It had had to. Because
the population of the area had increased
enormously—some thirty- or forty-fold.

Forcing the development of such
innovations as irrigation and the use of
the plow.

Every year, more and more land was
being put under cultivation. It had to be.
To support a population always one step
ahead of food production.

It was wonderful.

But there was even more than that to
gladden God's heart. The box of keys that had
been unlocked with the key of agriculture
was wide open. Egypt and Mesopotamia
and the Indus valley were blossoming with
cities: Mohenjo-daro and Ur and Susa and
Memphis and Heracleopolis and Coptos and
others. A trade route two thousand miles long
carried the goods of wealth and power and

technology: copper, silver, gold, and ivory. Literacy was well established, and the foundations of geometry and mathematics were being laid.

There could be no question about it now. Man was at last worth consorting with.

At last worthy of divine friendship.

Divine guidance.

Enlightenment.

It was time at last.

For God to begin to reveal Himself to man.

This is the way *Homo magister* likes to tell the story.

His is a fastidious God.

A God who, understandably, did not care to associate with the wrong sort of people. With savages.

He was saving Himself.

For people of His own class.

The ruling class.

Homo magister has a right to tell the story this way. It's his own God he's talking about, after all.

But it's not the only way to tell it.

I like to think, outrageously, that I have a
better opinion of God than *Homo magister*
does.

That He is not a snob.

That He loved man from the beginning.

I like to think of Him that way.

It helps me think of Him that way if I
call Him something else.

The gods. They seem friendlier somehow.

Be outrageous with me.

Imagine that the gods did not bring man
into the world and snub him for three million
years.

Imagine that the gods, having shaped man
from the Australopithecines, did not despise
their own handiwork.

Imagine that they had a care for *Homo
habilis*, squat and dim and ugly as he was.

I suppose he was ugly. Ugly as a toad,
maybe. Be ridiculous.

Imagine that the gods loved *Homo habilis*
as much as they love toads.

Be totally absurd.

Imagine that the gods loved *Homo habilis* as much as they love insurance salesmen.

No, that's going too far.

That's unthinkable.

Stick with the toads.

Imagine that the gods loved *Homo habilis* as much as they love toads.

As much as they love crocodiles and weevils and jellyfish and coyotes and Gila monsters and porcupines and mice and elephants and sharks and crickets.

Be preposterous.

Imagine that the gods have a care for everything that lives in the community of life on earth.

Imagine that they had a care for *Homo habilis*.

Imagine something else preposterous.

That they actually realized that *Homo habilis* was human.

That they knew he was different from a sparrow or a spider or a beaver.

61

That they understood as well as we
do what being human means.

Not just intelligence.

There's more to it than that.

It isn't just that man is smarter than
sparrows or spiders or beavers.

Man does something they don't do,
can't do.

He learns things they can't learn.

And what he learns he teaches to his
children.

And what his children learn they teach
to their children.

There is an accumulation, generation
after generation. An accumulation called
culture. It includes everything. Knowledge
about the world, about people, about the past,
about how to behave, about how to solve
problems, about how to do things and make
things; it includes songs, stories, theories,
beliefs, superstitions, prejudices.

Everything.

Culture just sort of goes along with
intelligence.

With intelligence of a human order.

When you have intelligence of a human order, it just automatically produces an accumulation of knowledge, generation after generation.

You might even say that culture is innate to man.

Just think.

Man was not born a civilization-builder. That's a fact.

But he *was* born a culture-builder.

Stretch yourself.

Imagine that the gods were as clever as I am.

That they knew that man was a culture-builder.

Imagine that this didn't take them by surprise.

That they were prepared to cope with culture-builders.

That they knew how to take care of culture-builders as well as they knew how to take care of nest-builders and web-builders and dam-builders.

Try to imagine the gods being as competent as that.

It's hard, I know, to imagine such a thing. *Homo magister* has trained us to imagine God so differently. To imagine that He is really at a loss to know what to do with man.

That there seems to be some problem there between God and man, and God can't seem to figure out how to lick it.

He tries this, He tries that. Everything seems to work a little. But nothing seems to work very much. Nothing seems to produce the desired result.

Which isn't always entirely clear.

It's difficult. But try to imagine that the gods I'm talking about were not baffled to know what to do with man.

Go a bit further.

Imagine that the community of life being shaped in the hands of the gods was as well prepared for the appearance of culture-builders as it had been for the appearance of nest-builders.

Imagine that the community was as well shaped to be the home of culture-builders as it had been to be the home of web-builders or dam-builders.

Try to imagine that the gods knew their business to that extent.

That too I know is hard.

Homo magister has trained us to imagine that the world as it was—as God made it— was a wretched home for man. An entirely inappropriate and inadequate home for man.

Even hostile to man.

It was, in fact, a rotten place to live, as God made it.

Not a home at all.

It was a jungle.

A home for apes. Not a home for man.

It was a bungled job.

God made the world for man, but He bungled it.

Man himself had to put it right. Had to take over the job himself.

Had to build his own home.

His true home.
Away from that jungle.

It's hard, I know. But try.
Try to imagine something different
from that. Gods who were not bunglers.
Gods who knew their business.
Gods who knew what they were doing.
With the world.
With man.

If you can't imagine it, ask an anthropologist.
He or she will tell you something outrageous.
That our ancestors were well adapted to live
in the world as the gods made it. That the
world was well shaped to be the home of
man.
He or she will tell you something even
worse. That people who live the way our
ancestors lived have an easier time staying
alive than we do.
Much easier.
They expend less time and energy getting
the things they need than we do. And they all
get them—not just the lucky or the talented

or the ruthless or the determined.

They are the most leisured and best fed group on earth.

Don't take my word for it. Ask an anthropologist.

Imagine that the gods knew that *Homo habilis* was man.

And that they knew that man is a culture-builder.

Imagine that they had a care for him.

That they were glad to see him when he arrived.

That they weren't baffled to know what to do with him.

That they knew what a culture-builder needs.

Imagine something damnable.

That they wanted *Homo habilis* to live.

As they had wanted lions to live, and seals and hyenas and water buffalo and sunflowers.

They wanted him to live: short, ugly, and dim *Homo habilis*. Not just for ten thousand

years, like *Homo magister*. They wanted
him to live for hundreds of thousands of
years, for millions of years.

In which to be shaped in their hands.
As all who live are shaped.
They wanted him to live in their hands.
Not like *Homo magister*, who took his
life into his own more competent hands,
and now, after just a few thousand years,
is facing death.

They wanted him to live in their hands.
And be what he was. A culture-builder.

He needed a law.

Just one.
Just one that would keep him living in
their hands. That would prevent him from
taking his life out of their hands.

They wanted life for *Homo habilis*.
Millions of years of it.

And so he needed a law.

Just the one law, to keep him living in
their hands.

One law to be incorporated into whatever

cultures he might build.

Just the one law to be the basis for all his cultural experiments.

And of course he would experiment.

Just as birds experiment with nests.

How else was he to learn?

How else was he to become more of what we mean by human except by experimenting?

He would make mistakes. Of course he would make mistakes.

They wouldn't hurt him. So long as he lived in their hands.

He had time to try everything.

Living in their hands.

He could try building patriarchal cultures and matriarchal cultures and patriarchal-matrilineal cultures and matriarchal-patrilineal cultures. He could try building monogamous cultures and polygamous cultures and monandrous cultures and polyandrous cultures and monogynous cultures and polygynous cultures. He could try building cultures in which the idea was to be generous and helpful and compassionate and cooperative. He could try building

cultures in which the idea was to be cold
and haughty and selfish and nasty.

None of that mattered.

Cultures that gave people a good life
would continue and grow, and cultures that
didn't would disappear. Just the way
successful species continue and grow, and
others don't.

Homo's cultural mistakes couldn't hurt
him.

So long as he lived in their hands.

There was only one mistake that could hurt
him.

Only one mistake that he must not use as
the foundation for any culture.

Only one mistake that had to be forbidden
to him: taking his life out of their hands.

Taking his life into his own hands.

Because that mistake would be deadly to
man.

That mistake would mean death for man.

He needed just the one law.

One law. The basis for a thousand

cultures. A million cultures.

Because, for some crazy reason, the gods love diversity.

Never make two things alike.

"Good heavens," one of the gods said when he saw that man had awakened to life in the community of life. "How are we to frame the one law young *Homo* needs to know in order to live a billion years?"

"That's only half of it," another says. "Assuming we can figure out how to frame such a law, how are we to teach it to him?"

Terrible problems.

The gods scratch their heads.

One offers a suggestion:

"Young *Homo* has a fairly adequate sort of language, I understand. Why don't we learn that language, and then, when we've written the law, we can translate it into his language for him."

The others nod enthusiastically.

But one of them says, "Wait a bit. You know very well what sort of limitations human language has. You can't say anything in it that means absolutely one thing and only one thing and nothing else."

"That's true," the others agree gloomily.

"Anything whatever you say in human language is subject to interpretation, to being fiddled with and twisted this way and that."

"I'm afraid," says another, nodding, "that if you lined up a thousand humans and said something very simple like "Thou shalt not kill," you'd get a hundred thousand different interpretations of what it means. For that matter, even I don't know what it means, now that I've put it into human language."

They tug on their beards moodily.

They wring their hands hopelessly.

Imagine something different from that. Gods who were not bunglers.

Gods who knew their business.

Gods who knew how to take care of culture-builders as well as they knew how to take care of hive-builders and burrow-builders.

Gods who knew how to give man what he needed.

A law was in readiness.

It had already been written.
　　It had been written billions of years before.
　　Where the gods write what they write.

You know where the gods write what they write.
　　Not on clay tablets or papyrus; I'm not talking about bunglers here. I'm talking about competent gods. Gods who shaped a universe that has worked for fifteen billion years. You know where they write what they write.
　　You know where they wrote the law of gravity.
　　In the fabric of matter itself.
　　It was written there from the beginning.
　　It lay hidden there, where it was written, for fifteen billion years. It was unnoticed. Unthought of.
　　Yet obeyed.
　　No one even guessed it was there.
　　Until one day someone—someone sitting

(at least in fancy) under an apple tree—
watched an apple fall to the ground. He
looked dumbfounded at the apple. At the
ground. His jaw dropped. "Good Lord," he
said, "it's a law. When we walk we are
following a law."

And, realizing that the law was a law,
he changed the course of history.

The law I'm talking about is a law like that.

A fundamental law of the biological
community.

As the law of gravity is a fundamental law
of matter.

It's written in the very fabric of the living
community.

As the law of gravity is written in the very
fabric of matter. Written there in the living
community from the very beginning of life.

It lay hidden there, where it was written,
for four billion years. It was unnoticed.

Unthought of.

Yet obeyed.

No one even guessed it was there.

Until one day someone—someone sitting

(at least in fancy) beside the carcass of a deer—watched the flies swarming over it. Dumbfounded, he looked at the deer. At the flies. His jaw dropped. "Good Lord," he said, "it's a law. When we live we are following a law."

Realizing that the law was a law, he might have changed the course of history.

If he had been a member of *Homo magister*.

If the discoverer of this law had been a member of *Homo magister*, he (or perhaps she) would have rocked the civilized world.

And won himself a rich damnation.

The damnation that fell on the heads of Copernicus and Darwin would have seemed like benedictions compared to the damnation that would have fallen on his. The Nobel Prize committee might have detested him, but they could not have withheld the accolade.

His name would now be a household word, like Freud or Darwin or Einstein.

But he wasn't a member of *Homo magister*. Or she wasn't.

He, or she, was an Ihalmiut Eskimo living in one of the most remote and barren areas on earth: the Great Barrens of Canada.

All the members of this small, modest people knew that the law was a law by the time *Homo magister* got around to them. They thought nothing of it, no more than we think of the law of gravity.

It seemed obvious to them. The way the law of gravity seems obvious to us.

They spoke of it in passing to *Homo magister*, to explain why they lived as they did. To explain why they didn't care to live as he did.

He smiled and patted them on the head.

They were only savages, after all. They hadn't gone to the right schools, hadn't read the right books. They didn't know the history, philosophy, theology, biology, physics, and anthropology they needed to know in order to make *Homo magister* recognize that what they'd discovered was a law.

The law was more than all of those things to them. It was sublime poetry. And so they spoke to *Homo magister* in poetry. And so he smiled and patted them on the head.

And then he destroyed them.

They called it the Law of Life. It sounds almost too good to be true, but that's what they called it. It really couldn't have been called anything else, any more than the law of gravity could be called anything else.

It is the Law of Life.

Followed everywhere—in the seas, on the shores, in the forests, in the ponds, on the plains, in the deserts.

Followed by everything that moves in the community of life—great and small, naked and armored, scaled and feathered, spined and spineless, brainy and brainless—by paramecia and elephants and sharks and grasshoppers and frogs and wolves and ticks and deer and rabbits and turtles and owls.

It's a universal law.

Written where only the gods could have written it.

In the fabric of the living community.

And so a law was in readiness for *Homo habilis.*

A single law.

A biological law. But not merely a biological law.

A sublime law.

The pattern for a million cultures, no two alike.

As it is the pattern for a million species, no two alike.

A law good enough to be the basis for a billion years of cultural experimentation.

A law never to be outworn or outgrown.

Because it had been written by gods who were actually gods. And not blunderers.

A law was in readiness for man as he was.

It didn't have to be taught to him—any more than it has to be taught to butterflies or jackals or tadpoles.

Any more than the law of gravity had to be taught to him.

He was born following it.

As the community of life itself had been born following it.

He didn't wonder what law it was he was following when he lived. Any more than he wondered what law he was following when he walked.

The law was in readiness for the life of man.

The one law that would keep him where life was. In the community of life being shaped in the hands of the gods.

It was the law of membership in that community.

The general law of the community.

To be followed by all.

So that all could have life.

The law was in readiness for man the culture-builder. The only law he had to incorporate into every culture he might build. As it is the only law that must be incorporated into every nest that birds might build, into every web that spiders might build, into every dam that beavers might build.

Because it is the law that fosters life.

It was easy to follow. As easy to follow as the law of gravity.

And following it over thousands of millennia, cultures of unthinkable diversity appeared throughout the community of man, were tested, were shaped, were abandoned, were refined.

No two alike, as the gods seem to like things.

No two alike, except for one thing only: that they were founded on the Law of Life. The law whose only restraint was to keep man living in the hands of the gods.

In the hands of gods who knew their business.

Gods who knew how to foster life for culture-builders as well as they'd known how to foster life for the world.

Strange gods.

Strange to *Homo magister*.

Strange to him because they love all whom they call to life and not just him.

Strange to him because they wanted *life* for man—not *power*.

Strange to him because they're competent to rule the world—without man's help.

They're strange to him for another reason.

Because they're not fussing over him. Not pleading with him to repent. Not begging him to return the rule of the world to them.

They don't have to.

It will be returned to them.

You see, the Law of Life has sanctions that protect the community of life. Sanctions that protect it from those who imagine that they can live as no others live: by defying the law.

Sanctions for outlaws.

Outlaws become extinct.

Made in the USA
Lexington, KY
05 February 2017